WRITTEN BY
CHRISTINE LAZIER AND MARIE FARRE,
BEATRICE FONTANEL, PATRICK GEISTDORFER, ANDRE LUCAS,
PIERRE PFEFFER, BERNARD PLANCHE, PENNY STANLEY-BAKER

ILLUSTRATED BY
JOELLE BOUCHER, LAURA BOUR,
CHRISTIAN BROUTIN, BERNARD DAGAN, DONALD GRANT,
PIERRE DE HUGO, ANNE LOGVINOFF, RENE METTLER, DANIEL MOIGNOT,
CLAUDE AND DENISE MILLET, JEAN-MARIE POISSENOT,
FRANCK STEPHAN, PIERRE-MARIE VALAT, DIZ WALLIS

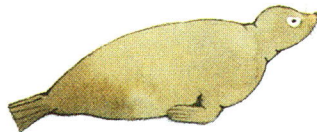

TRANSLATED AND ADAPTED BY
ANGELA ROYSTON AND GHISLAINE NOUVION SEVERS
WITH SARAH GIBSON, SARAH MATTHEWS
AND PENNY STANLEY-BAKER

We gratefully acknowledge the advice of:
Sarah Heath, M. Phil Conservation Policy,
Dr Jane Mainwaring, Steve Pollock,
Andy Ottaway, Wildlife Campaigner, Greenpeace

Cover design by Peter Bennett

ISBN 1 85103 178 2
© 1991 by Editions Gallimard
English text © 1993
by Moonlight Publishing Ltd
First published in Great Britain 1993 by Moonlight Publishing Ltd,
36 Stratford Road, London W8
Printed in Italy by Editoriale Libraria

ANIMALS OF THE WILD

CONTENTS

MOONLIGHT PUBLISHING

Polar bears live in the icy Arctic.

You are not likely to meet the animals in this book, at least not in the wild. Many of them live in inaccessible places, in the frozen, polar wastes or hidden deep in the jungle or the sea. Animals avoid people, because people can invade their territory* and threaten them. But in this book you can get to know animals without disturbing them.

Let's begin with a visit to the Arctic, that frozen, windswept continent around the North Pole.

Polar bears are determined hunters.
They have to be. Food is scarce in the barren wastes of the Arctic. Yet polar bears are the biggest meat-eaters of all. Males can weigh three times as much as a full-grown lion. Some even weigh 700 kilos!
Polar bears prey* mainly on seals and walruses. They lie in wait on the ice and then catch seals when they come up to the surface to breathe.

Where do polar bears spend the winter?
Females escape the bitter winds by digging a deep den under the snow. Their cubs are born there. Males, however, only take shelter if the weather is very bad.
The cubs are growing bigger.
At birth they are the size of a rat and weigh under one kilo. But they grow quickly on their mother's milk which is full of fat. By the time they are three months old they weigh 10 kilos.
The female leaves her den in March or April. She takes her cubs with her and they learn to hunt for baby seals. They will stay with their mother until they are just over two years old. Then, like other polar bears, they will live on their own.

Their fat, furry bodies keep them warm.

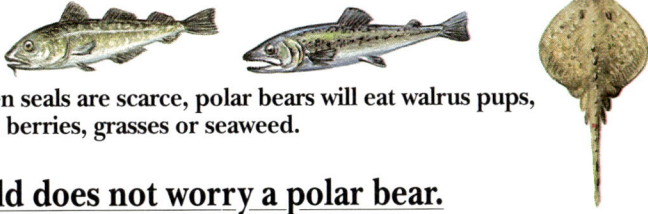

When seals are scarce, polar bears will eat walrus pups, fish, berries, grasses or seaweed.

Arctic foxes, walruses and reindeer are also hunted by polar bears.

Cold does not worry a polar bear.

They are well protected by a warm fur coat, and, under that, a thick layer of fat.
They can swim for hours in the frozen seas. How do they manage to walk and even run on the ice without slipping? The underside of their paws is covered with hair which gives them a good grip on the ice.

Polar bears may come to town.

In winter, while the pregnant females stay in their dens, the males search for food and may follow the seals southwards. The bears may pursue the smell of food right up to the houses, terrifying the people there. Then the bears are trapped, put to sleep, and airlifted by helicopter back to the ice.

Seals live in the cold waters of the northern seas.

Seals are excellent swimmers

but they are mammals*, like us. They have to come to the surface to breathe in air. In winter, when the sea is frozen, they make breathing holes in the ice.

There are many kinds of seal.

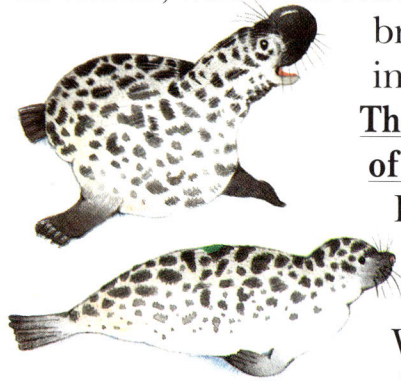

Hooded seals have a kind of pocket on their heads. When they are excited, the pocket, or hood, fills up with air and their heads become twice as big. Hooded seals can weigh more than 400 kilos. Ringed seals are much smaller. They stay around or under the coastal ice and eat shellfish and small fish.

Hooded seals

Walruses live on land and in the sea.

Like seals, they give birth to their cubs on land. They are covered with short, sleek fur. You can recognize walruses by their long tusks.

Their tusks are their tools.

The walrus' tusks are just two long teeth. They use them as clamps to help them climb onto ice-floes*. They also use them to dig holes in the ice and to scrape the sea-bed for shellfish. They even fight with them.

Walruses

The Emperor penguin rules Antarctica.

Which other animals live in Antarctica?
Seals, sea-lions, elephant seals and many birds like penguins live there too.

Emperor penguins are very good fathers.
When the female has laid her egg, she carefully passes it to the male. He puts it on his feet and covers it with a special fold of skin to keep it warm. Then the female sets off across the ice back to the sea. The father incubates* the egg and looks after the young chick. He has not eaten since the end of summer.

The mother returns.
When the chick is about two months old, its mother returns with a crop full of fish for it. Now the father sets off for the sea. He has lost a third of his body weight and is weak. He too returns with food for the chick. While their parents are away, the chicks huddle together in a group until they are big enough to journey to the sea and find food for themselves.

Has anyone ever said you're like a bear with a sore head? In fact it's not true that bears are bad-tempered. Brown bears are solitary and hate being disturbed but the smaller American black bears are quite docile. Both kinds live in the forests and tundra of northern Europe, North America and Asia.

You stand very little chance of meeting them!

Bears avoid people and all other animals, even each other. Males and females live apart, except for a short time in the spring when they come together to mate*.

What do brown bears eat?

Almost everything! They like plants, nuts, insects, grubs, fish and young animals. Like most bears, they love sweet food like wild honey. They eat all summer and get fat. Then they dig a hole to sleep in through the winter.

Grizzlies are the fiercest bears of all.

A young grizzly's first fight with a caribou

The huge grizzly is very strong.

When this big brown bear stands on its hind legs, it may be 3 metres high – as high as a room! They are called grizzlies because their fur often turns a grizzled grey colour, and because they are so fierce. Like all bears, grizzlies are curious. Campers watch out when they come sniffing round their tents. Grizzlies are very ready to attack.

Grizzlies like patrolling their territory*.

They live in the mountains and forests of Alaska, Canada and northern Siberia. Each bear has its own territory where it returns year after year. It patrols this stretch of land, scratching on trees and leaving its own special scent. These 'keep out' signals warn other grizzlies to stay away. Grizzlies eat berries and small animals, such as squirrels, but they'll attack caribou and bighorn sheep too. They will kill a large animal with several powerful blows. Then they hide the body under the trees and return to eat it later. Sometimes they chase bison, but they prefer to hunt young or wounded animals. Bison can run faster than the grizzly!

A grizzly bear is raiding a bees' nest for honey. The bear's thick fur protects it from the stings of the angry bees.

Black bears are smaller than brown bears.

Black bears don't have to feed themselves.

In the wildlife reserves of North America, they just wait for the tourists to come and feed them. But don't trust their friendly appearance. If you don't produce something to eat, they might just bite you instead! They are very good at sniffing out camp sites and stealing food.

Like all bears, black bears love swimming, and it helps to get rid of their fleas.

Black bears on the prowl for food. Wise campers store their food outside their tents.

One of the biggest bears is the kodiak.

It is a fierce brown bear which lives in Alaska. The males weigh up to 700 kilos.

Look at the bear's huge paws!

Bears walk and run on all fours. They have broad flat paws, like our feet. Each paw has five long curved claws, so it can be a terrible weapon. A bear can move at 35 kilometres an hour, as fast as a man.

It charges its victim and then stands on its hind legs to attack. It swipes its enemy with its front paws.

Bear cubs are born in winter.

They are born in the warm den their mother digs for them. By spring they are old enough to follow her outside when she hunts for food. She teaches them to dig up roots and pick berries. She shows them how to open an ants' nest with their claws. They learn to swim and catch fish. They climb trees to get fruit and raid birds' nests. The cubs stay with their mother until they are 18 months old. Then they must start life on their own.

Lynxes and wolves prowl through prairies and forests.

Lynxes are wild cats.

In North America lynxes live in forests. But in Asia, Europe and America red lynxes live among the rocks, in marshlands and even in deserts.

The lynx is nocturnal and prowls through its territory* alone.

Each lynx marks out its own area with urine and droppings. Their smell tells other lynxes to keep away. Their dappled fur helps them to hide among the trees and rocks.

Lynx

Wolverines hunt for big meals!

They live in northern coniferous* forests, and they are so strong they are capable of killing animals larger than themselves. In winter, wolverines hunt large reindeer and caribou, but they will also eat berries.

Wolverine

The howls of wolves drift over prairies* and forests.

Wolves have different cries: growling, snarling, barking and howling. When they hunt at night, they howl to keep in touch with each other and keep the pack together in the dark.

Millions of bison and pronghorn once roamed the prairies.

But in the last century they were hunted almost to extinction* by American settlers. The remaining herds are protected by law and graze in national parks.

Pronghorns

The three-toed sloth spends most of its life hanging upside-down at the top of a tree.

The Amazon is a huge river which flows across South America. On either side stretches a vast tropical rainforest*. Walking through it, you may think it is uninhabited, but in fact there are thousands of animals all around you.

The rainforest is hot and damp. Many trees grow as high as a ten-storey building. Thousands of animals live in the rainforest but they are hard to see because they hide in the trees.

Jaguars hunt on the dark forest floor.

They weigh more than 200 kilos and are too heavy to climb trees. When they are two months old, the young learn to hunt with their mother, hiding in the shadows and pouncing on their prey*.

Ocelots are hunted by jaguars and by people.

The adults are too big to be attacked by boa constrictors and caymans, but their cubs are often killed. When a male and female ocelot walk together through the forest, they miaow to each other like cats. They are sometimes known as "tiger cats" or "jaguar cats".

Ocelot

A peccary is a small wild boar with skinny legs.

They live in packs of up to a hundred pigs. Each animal has a special gland* on its bottom which produces a smelly and oily secretion. They recognize each other's smell and use it to mark their territory*. When a peccary is attacked it will chatter its teeth. The noise is so loud it can be heard far away.

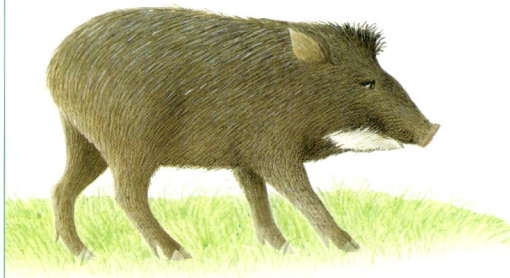

Peccary

Tribes of small monkeys leap from tree to tree.

The steamy, leafy tropical* forest is the kingdom of the small monkeys. They leap among the tree-tops in noisy, chattering clans.

This uakari has a bald head. When it gets excited it goes red in the face.

Squirrel monkeys chase each other through the trees.

They are so quick and agile they appear and disappear among the branches as if by magic. They never leave the trees.

Golden lion tamarins are very rare.

Night monkey

Monkeys use their long tails to help them balance. That is why they do not fall out of the trees.

Which is the only monkey that stays awake at night? It is the night monkey. Its enormous eyes help it to see in the dark.

Squirrel monkeys

Woolly monkeys are tamed by the Indians.

Marmoset

The pygmy marmoset is the smallest monkey in the world.

You could easily fit one into your pocket. It grips the trees with tiny, curved claws.

Snakes poison or squeeze their prey to death.

A tree boa is well camouflaged*.
With its emerald green skin and white stripes you would not notice it among the leaves. It lies quite still, waiting to attack a bird or lizard. Like other boas, it coils itself around its victim then squeezes it to death. When it wants to rest, it just twists its long body around a branch.

Scarlet macaw

A rattlesnake kills with a poisonous bite. Its fangs inject venom into its prey. Rattlesnakes swallow their food whole.

Anacondas are the biggest snakes.
They are just over 9 metres long. They swim in the river and attack animals which come there to drink.
A female can lay as many as 30 or 40 eggs in one go.

A jaguar prowls by the river. It will even attack the sharp-toothed cayman. The bird-eating spider is also on the lookout for prey*.

16

Red ibis

Toucan

Jacamar

Jacamar

Anaconda

South American macaws are the most colourful parrots in the world.

The scarlet macaw is also one of the world's biggest birds. Parrots live in large, noisy flocks, except when it is time to mate*.

The toucan's large beak is full of holes.

This makes it light. It is made of a bony substance which is hard and colourful on the outside. Although their beaks are so bulky, toucans use them skilfully to pick fruit, and to catch lizards, frogs and small chicks.

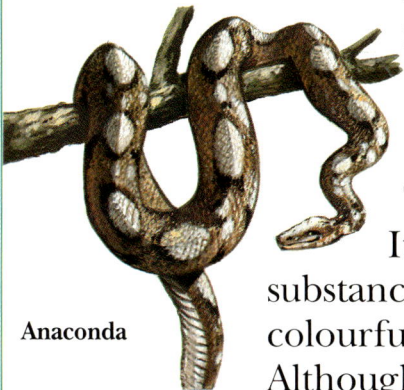

Flocks of birds feed together.

While some birds chase insects high in the trees, the jacamar perches on a low branch and waits for moths and butterflies. It snatches them from the air in full flight and hits them against a branch to kill them.

The red ibis is prized for its beautiful feathers.

Although it is protected by law, it is still hunted. But the biggest threat to all the animals of the rainforest* is the destruction of the forest itself. As the trees are felled, the birds lose their food and shelter.

Life is harsh in the high mountains of the Andes.

Mountains are inhospitable places.

The higher you climb the colder and windier it gets. The air is thinner: there is less oxygen* for plants and animals to breathe. Only a few small plants can grow here. Amazingly, many kinds of animals do live in the high Andes mountains of South America. They include insects, birds, vicunas and guanacos. Lower down, in the warm, wet forests, live many other animals, such as the spectacled bear.

Alpaca

Llama

Vicuna

No two spectacled bears look alike!

Each has a different pattern of white fur around its eyes. This gentle animal lives on its own or with its family. It eats mainly fruit such as figs and the young shoots of palm trees. It feeds at night and sleeps during the day in a nest built from broken branches. Spectacled bears are very suspicious of people. People have cut down trees to build roads and helped to destroy their habitat*. People hunt them because they sometimes attack llamas when they are very hungry. Spectacled bears are now an endangered species*. There are fewer than 4,000 of them left in the world.

Vicunas, guanacos, alpacas and llamas are related to camels.

They are smaller than camels and because their feet are narrower and firmer they can walk on steep mountainous tracks. Llamas and alpacas are now reared by people for their long, woolly hair.

Watch out for the guanaco's spit!

Guanaco

Guanacos live in small groups. In the mating season, the males fight fiercely over the females. They get very excited and spit a mixture of saliva and stomach juices into each other's faces.

Vicunas live 4,000 metres high.

They live in family groups of a male with two or three females and their young. The male marks out their territory* with his urine and droppings. In spring, each female has a baby. When a young male is a year old, he joins a group of other young males. Three years later, when he is an adult, he wanders off alone to look for his own females. Long ago, vicunas were hunted by the Incas. Only the Emperor of the Incas was allowed to wear a cape of vicuna wool. Today vicunas are a protected species*.

Condors and pumas look out for prey below them.

A puma is an agile mountain cat.
It likes to perch on a rocky peak and wait for its unsuspecting prey* to pass below. Then it pounces. Pumas hunt young stags, guanacos, rabbits, coyotes and lynxes. They are so strong they can carry an animal up to five times their own weight. They also catch large insects, snakes and sometimes even fish.

The female is pregnant for three months. Then she looks for a sheltered place at the bottom of a cliff to give birth. She feeds the cubs on her milk and looks after them on her own. When they are two and a half months old she starts to teach them how to hunt. When they are a year or two old they leave her to live on their own.

The condor is a huge bird of prey*. It soars by day in the wind among the peaks of the Andes. Then it swoops down onto its prey which may be as large as a calf. It also eats the flesh of dead mammals.

African savannas* are large plains with few trees, but plenty of grass when it rains. Many large mammals* live here: antelopes, giraffes, buffaloes and elephants.

Elephants are the biggest animals that walk the earth. Some adult males are as tall as the first storey of a house.

Elephants are the heaviest animals that live on land: one elephant can weigh as much as 100 adult people! But although they are so big, elephants move gently and quietly. With their colossal size, their strength and their wisdom, they live without fear. Who would dare to attack them? Even a hunting lion moves out of their way. Elephants eat plants and attack other living creatures only when they feel threatened.

An elephant's trunk can do almost everything.

The African elephant is bigger than the Indian elephant.

Elephants spend all day and most of the night eating.

They sleep for only about four hours a day! A full-grown elephant can eat 150 kilos of leaves, grass, fruit and roots a day. Sometimes they push over a whole tree just to reach the leaves. They often eat earth to get the minerals* they need and they have to drink a lot of water too: 70-90 litres each day!

What is a tool, a hand, a pump, a snorkel, and a nose all in one?

An elephant's trunk! It is made of muscle and has no bones. It is hollow and ends in sensitive lips. Thanks to its trunk, an elephant can breathe, pick fruit, and throw a lion into the air! It can use it to drink and to shower itself with water – a great delight in the hot sun. If an elephant swims under water, it can hold its trunk above the surface to allow it to breathe.

It is a trumpet too.

When an elephant calls out you can hear it for miles around! And it lifts its trunk in the air to sniff out danger and water.

Walking for water

For many months of the year there is no rain and the grasslands become very dry. Then the elephants move towards the forests, where there are always leaves for them to eat and water for them to drink. Once the rains come, the elephants move back onto the plains where the fresh green grass has begun to grow.

An elephant can easily walk 30 kilometres a day, swinging along on its enormous thick-skinned feet.

Elephants have sensitive skins and strong tusks.

Did you know that elephants have very thin, sensitive skin?

Sharp grasses scratch them, tsetse flies and ticks bite them and suck their blood.
To protect themselves, elephants roll in mud. As the mud dries, it cakes into a sort of armour.
Sometimes elephants spray themselves with dust as well.
A little bird, called a tick-bird, helps by picking off the pests and eating them.

What are tusks for?

Elephants can use their tusks for fighting, but they are also used for taking the bark off trees, for grubbing up roots, and for digging into damp sand to find drinking water.
Other animals like giraffes and rhinos share the water the elephants find.
Elephants are usually either right-tusked or left-tusked! Their tusks grow all their lives, and can be 3 metres long and weigh up to 100 kilos.
If one of the tusks crumbles or breaks it can become infected. This is very painful and makes the elephant aggressive.

An elephant has strong teeth.

It has four flat molars for grinding up the plants it eats. As one tooth wears down a new tooth pushes through to replace it.
In all, an elephant has six sets of teeth.
Each tooth weighs up to 5 kilos and is about 50 centimetres long!

This elephant is digging with its tusks to find water.

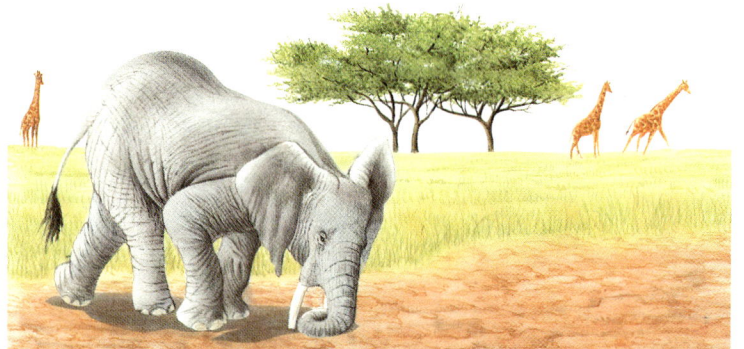

What a big baby!

A baby elephant is born!

It weighs 120 kilos, and is covered in soft, reddish hair. It has been growing inside its mother for nearly two years.

The mother dries her newborn baby and cuddles it with her trunk. Then she kicks it gently to help it stand up and lifts it with her trunk.
The other females of the herd sniff the new baby to get to know it too.

A baby does not use its trunk for the first few months, so it reaches for its mother's nipples with its mouth. It can drink 10 litres of milk a day.

Cuddled, pampered and protected

When it is only two days old, the baby elephant can walk along with the other elephants. It holds its mother's tail so it cannot get lost. The herd protects it and the baby suckles from other females as well as its mother. They help it to cross rivers and climb hills by supporting it round the middle with their trunk.

Young elephants grow quickly.

The baby feeds from its mother for about a year. When it is three months old it also starts to eat adult food. The baby learns how to use its trunk to pull up grass and pick acacia fruit. Until its own teeth are strong enough, the mother mashes the grass and leaves before putting them in the baby's mouth. Young male elephants stay with the herd until they are about ten years old. Females stay all their lives.

Elephants live in large herds.

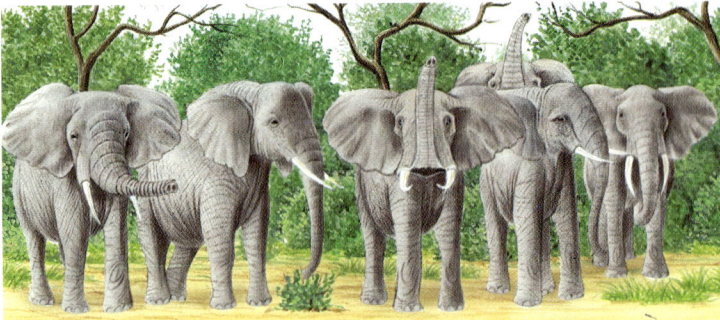

The leader of the herd is the oldest female.

Every herd is a large family made up of a female, her sisters and daughters and their children of all ages. The leader is the oldest and the wisest. She knows where food is to be found at different seasons of the year. She knows where to find water. And she knows where there is danger.

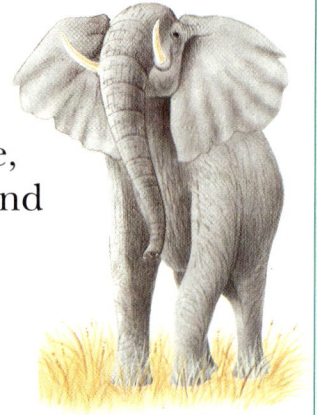

The other females learn from her and follow wherever she goes. When she dies, the next oldest female takes over as leader.

Elephants are very affectionate to each other.

They never quarrel. They touch and stroke each other with their trunks. Each elephant has its own place in the herd. Although they push against each other, they are only pretending to fight. If a baby elephant is upset, a female puts the end of her trunk into its mouth to comfort it.

Elephants are noisy eaters.

They make gurgling noises as they eat, rather like the rumblings our stomachs sometimes make. This 'concerto' allows them to keep in touch when they can't see each other. They also make other sounds too low for us to hear.

We must protect the elephants.

Male elephants live in smaller groups.
When they are about ten years old, young males begin to get on the females' nerves and so they leave their mother's herd. At first they join a group of other young males, but as they get older, they go off on their own. At mating time, a male elephant gets very excited. A thick, smelly liquid runs down his cheeks from a gland* between his ears and eyes. He follows a female until she allows him to mate* with her.
Male elephants fight to test their strength, but like humans they will gather round to help the sick and dying. Even when an elephant has died, they will try to help it stand up.

Danger!
A female elephant sounds the alarm, trumpeting loudly through her trunk. She has spotted a lion. The others squeeze close together in a circle with the babies in the middle. The old cow-elephant pulls tufts of grass and throws them to the lion. Then she moves forward, ears flapping and tusks forward.

African elephants are under threat.
People kill elephants for their ivory tusks. Since 1989 it has been illegal to sell or buy ivory, but elephant poaching still goes on.

Zebras live in constant danger.

Their stripes help to disguise them as they graze* among the shrubs, but they are prey* to lions, hyenas, leopards and cheetahs. They can't go more than three days without drinking water. Leopards often wait for them to come and drink at a waterhole*. Zebras live in family groups, a male with his females and their young. When the male is 16 to 18 years old, he is pushed out by a younger male who then takes his place.

Antelopes

Buffaloes are Africa's wild cattle.

They can be fierce. They can charge a lion and rip it open with their horns. But when they are chased by an elephant they will gallop away as fast as they can! Buffalo are said to be irritable and dangerous, but they will not charge unless injured.

Have you ever heard hyenas laughing?

It means they have found some exciting prey. Hyenas are the scavengers of the African grasslands, and feed on dead animal carcasses*, but when in a group, they will also attack live animals.

What a strange animal a warthog is!

Its head is covered with warts. It has two long canine teeth which stick up either side of its snout. They are useful for digging up roots, bulbs and tubers to eat.

The warthog also eats grass, fruit and bark and sometimes catches small rodents*.

It makes its home in an abandoned burrow or in an old termite* or porcupine nest. When it is threatened it sticks up its tail and runs away with its family close behind!

Warthog

The giraffe looks down from a great height!

How does a giraffe drink with such a long neck?
With difficulty! It spreads its front legs wide apart then swings its neck up and down, faster and faster until its mouth reaches the water. It drinks up to 15 litres of water at a time.

A giraffe can see for miles around.
Because it is almost 6 metres tall, it can see a lion creeping through the grass long before the antelopes, zebras and other grassland animals.

A giraffe spends half the day eating. It munches leaves, small branches, pods and acacia fruit. It finds the tastiest morsels by looking and smelling. It feels for the softest fruit with its sensitive, hairy lips. Its black tongue, covered in slime, reaches through the branches to find soft twigs. The inside of its mouth is hard so it cannot be hurt by sharp thorns.

Giraffes watch out for each other.
They often graze* in small groups, each giraffe scanning a different part of the horizon, on the look-out for enemies.

A giraffe gives birth standing up...
and her baby falls 2 metres to the ground! The mother then licks the baby with her rough tongue to dry and rouse it. After an hour, the baby rises on its wobbly legs and follows its mother onto the grassland. It will grow by more than a metre in its first year.

Rhinos love mud.

Insects are their worst enemies.

A rhino's skin is thick, hard and rough, but it will do almost anything to avoid being stung by an insect! That is why it spends most of the day wallowing in muddy waters. When it gets out, the mud dries hard on its hide, and the insects cannot sting through this protective armour!
A rhinoceros weighs about 2 tonnes. Although it looks slow and heavy, it can run at 50 kilometres an hour. Its horn is made of keratin, just like your hair and nails.

Rhinos live in small groups.

Several rhinos share the same territory* which they mark with their urine and droppings. If an unknown male strays onto their land, he is immediately chased away. Rhinos feed on the leaves of small bushes. They always follow the same route and make a useful path for other animals through the thorn bushes.

A baby rhino has no horns. It weighs a hefty 40 kilos when it is born. It has been growing inside its mother for about 15 months.

The mother looks after her baby for two years. She protects it from hyenas.

Fierce, strong males rule tribes of baboons.

Baboons are strong and aggressive. Their long dog-like noses and sharp teeth make them fierce fighters. They live in big groups, or tribes, under the leadership of a dominant* male. Lookouts are posted to warn the group of danger.

Living in a baboon tribe

The strongest males lead the other males, the females and their offspring. They rule the group and defend it against any threat. When they see a leopard, a lion or a hyena, they bark loudly to warn others in the tribe.

Baboons eat almost everything.

They are omnivores*. They eat plants, lizards, insects, worms, scorpions and eggs. They will even devour newborn gazelles and antelopes.

The birth of a baby is a big event.

All the members of the baboon tribe want to stroke the baby! The mother is treated with great respect. The dominant* male comes and sits next to her.

At first baby baboons stay close to their mothers. After three months they begin playing with their friends.

At eight months the baby leaves its mother, but she will continue to protect it until it is two years old.

As soon as it is born, a baby can cling to its mother's fur and suckle her milk.

Gripping tightly to the fur on their mothers' tummies, the babies are carried about everywhere.

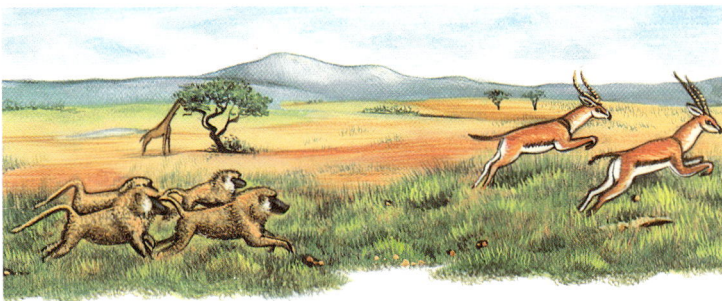

Baboons sometimes try to catch a young antelope.

When they are toddlers, they ride on their mothers' backs.

On the grasslands of Africa, the lion is king.

The lion tells everyone how important he is.
At dusk, as the last rays of sunshine turn everything red, the lion's roar is heard across the savanna*. He roars so loudly, he can be heard 8 kilometres away. He may roar to show off his strength or to express his pleasure after a good meal.

Lions live in a family group.
The pride is made up of two or three related males with their females and cubs. There may be up to thirty lions in a pride.

Male lions patrol their territory* and chase away lions from other prides. Females share the work of the pride, caring for the young and hunting.

Lions are said to be very lazy.
They sleep for 18 to 20 hours a day. When they rest, they lie against each other and yawn or snooze. Often, they lick themselves or rub their muzzles*.

At sunrise or sunset, the lionesses set off to hunt.
They look for easy prey* among a herd of zebras, gnus, antelopes or gazelles. They pick off an old or weak animal which cannot run as fast as the others.
The lioness has to leave behind her cubs when she hunts. They are then in great danger of attack, especially from hyenas.

The lioness teaches her cubs to hunt.

Many lions live in game reserves or national parks. Some reserves have hospitals for treating wounded and sick animals.

When the lions have recovered they are returned to the wild.

A perfectly planned attack

Lions are not fast runners so they tend to hunt as a team. When they find prey*, they surround it and creep up until they are close enough to attack. Then they pounce.

The lion's share

The male lions are the first to eat, then the females. Finally, the cubs are allowed to join in. Sometimes a cub is accidentally killed in the scuffle.

Lion cubs love to play and hunt.

Three months after mating, the lioness gives birth to two or three brown-spotted cubs. They will suckle* from their mother or one of her sisters until they are six months old. At three months they start eating meat too. The lioness teaches her cubs how to hunt when they are about eight months old. She will capture a small animal and let it loose near the cubs and then patiently help them chase and catch it.

Leopards lie hidden in the trees.

Look out for the leopard above your head!

During the day they sprawl along large branches. As they rest they keep an eye on their territory* below. At dusk they spring to the ground and prowl through the bushes looking for prey*: baboons, gazelles, hares and even lizards or snakes.

Cheetah

Leopards will attack anything!

Young monkeys, especially those that have strayed from their group, are common prey. Leopards sometimes steal into villages and attack lambs, chickens and dogs. They will also kill warthogs and antelopes twice their own size.

One killing bite

Like other big cats*, a leopard leaps on its prey and bites into its soft neck to strangle it. The prey cannot breathe and quickly dies. If the corpse* is too big to eat all at once, the leopard drags it up into a tree, out of the way of jackals, hyenas and lions. It will return later to finish its meal.

Have you heard of a caracal?

It looks like a small lynx but has yellow, fawn-coloured or reddish fur. It hunts hares, gazelles and small antelopes.
It lies in wait in the trees, or on a high rock, and then leaps. A caracal is so quick it can catch a bird in flight. It can even overpower an eagle!

Caracal

Cheetahs are built for speed.

They have small heads, flexible backs and long, powerful back legs. They are the only cats whose claws do not retract into their paws. Instead, their claws act like the studs on running shoes, gripping the ground as they run.

A cheetah's top speed is 110 kilometres per hour!

But it can maintain that speed for just a few seconds. If it hasn't caught its prey* in the first 200 metres, it must give up.

Females live separately from the males.

They live in small groups with their cubs. When the cubs are young, their mother hides them before she goes hunting. When she returns she feeds them with meat she has already chewed.

The mother cheetah keeps her cubs close to the trees, so they can quickly climb away from danger.

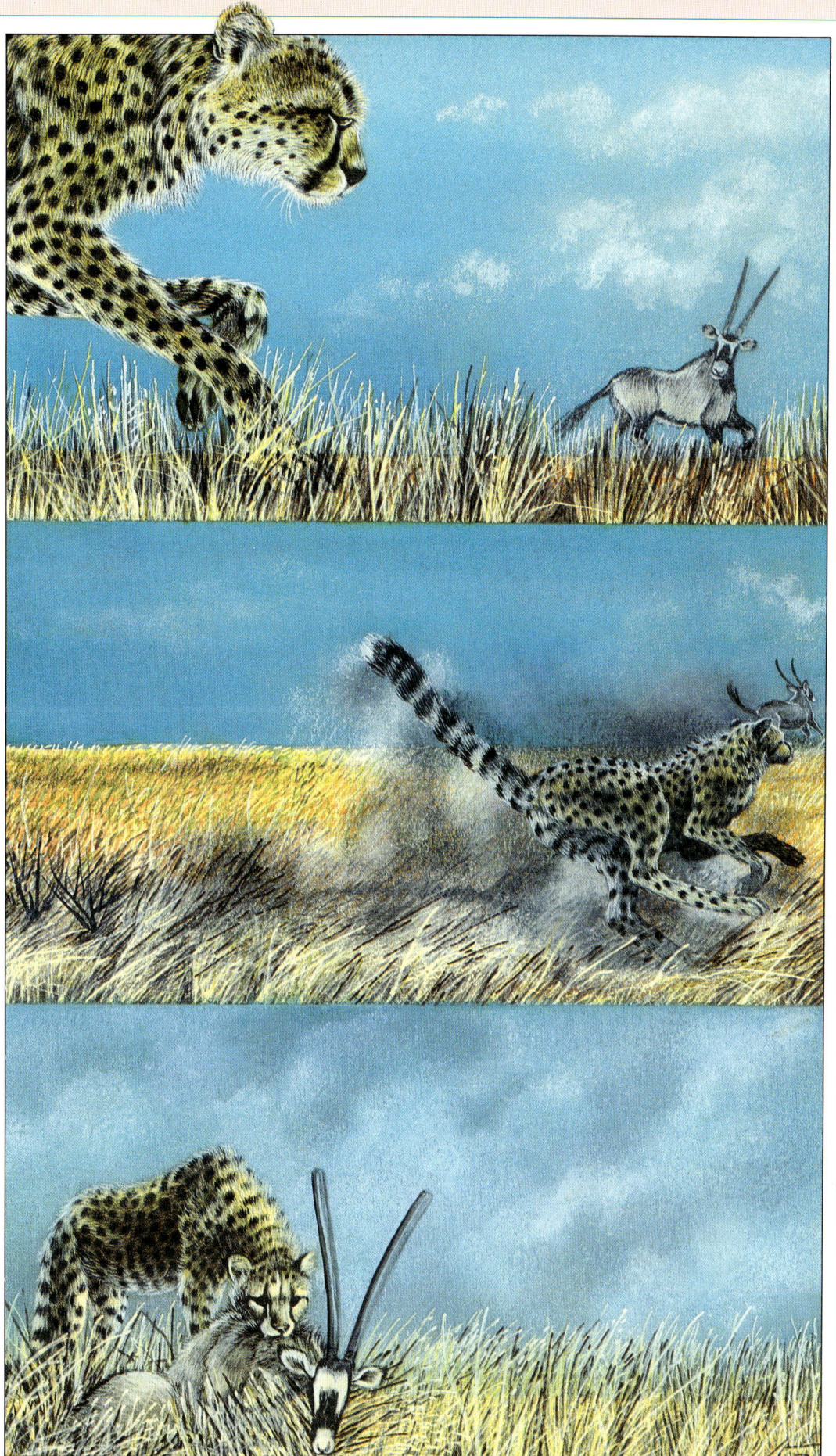

Crocodiles, hippos and brightly coloured birds...

The Nile is the longest river in the world but Africa also has other mighty rivers. They flow through deserts, jungles and grasslands. Many animals come to them to drink. But beware. A crocodile may be lying in wait beneath the murky surface!

River birds find plenty to eat.
Herons, egrets and ibis catch frogs, fish and insects. Geese and ducks graze* on the grass. Migrating* birds, such as storks and some teals, spend the winter in Africa.

Hippos love the water.
They spend all day in the river avoiding the hot sun. Where are the hippo's eyes, ears and nostrils? They are all on the top of its head, so it can see, hear and breathe without getting out of the water. A hippo has special valves which block off its ears and nostrils when it dives.

Hippos feed only at night.
When the sun goes down, the hippos wade out of the water and graze on the land. A hippo can eat 40 kilos of grass a night. You can see where they have been by the trail of droppings left behind!

What a yawn!
When a male hippo yawns, he is not tired. He is showing off his strong teeth to other males. Hippos fight fiercely over females and, as a result, they are often covered with scars.

Baby hippos are born under water.
The mother helps her baby come up to the surface to breathe. The baby suckles* under water but rides on its mother's back when she is swimming. At six months old, the baby hippo joins its mother feeding on the river bank.

Don't go swimming where the hippos wallow!
They may bite you with their long teeth,
which are razor-sharp .
A male controls a group of females
and he does not like people to go
near them. Females, too,
will chase you if they think
their young are in danger.
Hippos look clumsy on
land, but they move
easily and gracefully
in the water.

Crocodiles date back to the age of the dinosaurs.

Have you seen a crocodile?

They often look fast asleep in the zoo, but they can be so fierce that most other animals avoid them. Crocodiles live beside lakes and rivers in Africa, Asia, Australia and parts of America. At one time you would have found crocodiles in rivers all over Africa. But so many have been hunted for their skins, there are now many fewer.

Crocodiles are reptiles*

like snakes, tortoises and lizards. They have dry, scaly skin and they lay eggs on land. Crocodiles have several close relatives; alligators, caymans and gharials.

How can you tell if it is a crocodile?

By its large fourth tooth, which sticks out on each side of the lower jaw.

They are the most powerful reptiles in the world.

Crocodiles have existed since the time of the dinosaurs. The noise they make is called a bellow, though it sounds more like a groan. Did you know that there are some crocodiles four times as big as you, and over forty times heavier?

A crocodile's skin is as tough as armour.

It is made of scales, but it is not stiff like tortoise-shell. These scales fit beside each other and the skin moves and bends easily.

What are its weapons?

Its powerful tail and its strong jaws. A crocodile has 54 teeth. They fall out regularly but they are immediately replaced by new teeth.

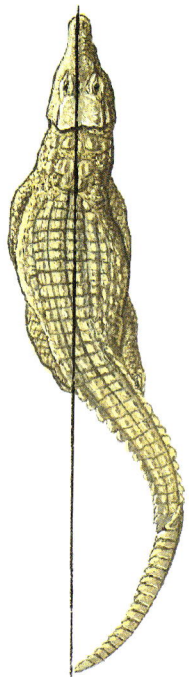

A crocodile swims by moving its tail. Only its eyes, ears and nostrils show above the water.

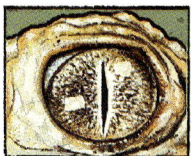 

In daylight   At night

A crocodile can see at night like a cat. The pupils of its eyes get wider in the dark.

Crocodiles swallow pebbles. These small stones help to break up the food which the crocodile has gulped down.

How do crocodiles move on land?

They crawl or trot, or sometimes glide on wet grass, pushing themselves along with their tail. If you ever find yourself being chased by a crocodile, run in zigzags. A crocodile can't turn easily, and this slows it down.

A dozen crocodiles can kill and eat a hippo.

One meal may last a crocodile a long time.

If it has to, a crocodile can go for two or three months without eating.

What other animals do crocodiles attack?

Young crocodiles hunt frogs and fish whereas the adults go for buffalo, zebra and gazelle. Sometimes they even attack elephants, but they only manage to bite their trunks. When they get old, crocodiles can be eaten by other crocodiles.

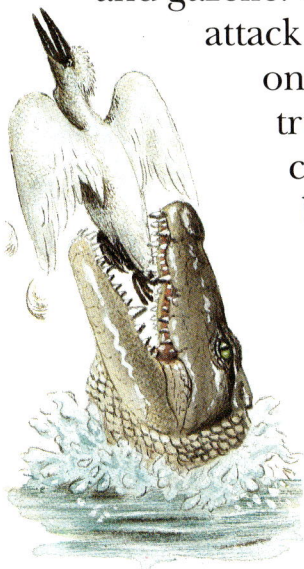

Crocodiles ambush their prey* at the water's edge.

You can see how a crocodile creeps up on a gazelle drinking from the river.

It knocks the gazelle into the water with its tail and jumps in after it. The crocodile drags the gazelle under water to drown it and then twists over and over, tearing off bits of flesh. A crocodile can't chew, so it swallows the pieces whole.

Crocodiles cannot live without water.

Plovers at work

Crocodiles have strange toothbrushes!

They are birds called plovers. The plovers peck off the leeches and bits of food that get stuck between the crocodile's teeth. Spur-winged plovers also help crocodiles by eating the ticks that live between their scales.

A crocodile can stay under water for two hours.

It closes its nostrils, so the water cannot get in. It has a special transparent eyelid to see underwater. Its ears are protected by a thin, waterproof skin which lets only sound through.

Why do crocodiles sleep in the water?

Like all reptiles*, crocodiles lose their body heat when the temperature drops. Because water retains the sun's heat longer than air, crocodiles spend the night under water. They crawl out at dawn. Then the sun makes the land warmer than the water, and they can lie on the bank basking in the sunshine.

After its meal, a crocodile will take a nap on the bank. If the sun is too hot, it will burrow into cool mud or open its huge mouth to let moisture evaporate* from the damp skin inside. This is how the crocodile cools down. If danger threatens, the plovers will give a warning cry, and the crocodile will dive below water.

Each group has its own territory*.

Crocodiles usually live in groups. The males mark the boundaries of their territory with a strong-smelling musk. This scent is made in a special gland* under their bellies.

The leader has the best spot on the river bank, the largest number of females and the biggest bits of meat. Old crocodiles lie on the soft grass, while the younger ones make do with the sloping banks.

Baby crocodiles live in a nursery.

How are crocodiles hatched?

The mother crocodile digs a nest with her front legs. It is shaped like a deep basket. In the nest she lays about 40 leathery, white eggs, the size of hens' eggs. Then she covers the nest with sand.

A baby crocodile weighs about 500 grams.

Many animals love to eat crocodiles' eggs!

While the eggs are incubating*, the mother seldom leaves the nest. If it is hot, she scurries down to the water for a dip, then lies over the nest to cool it down.
When the eggs are ready to hatch, after about three months, the baby crocodiles call out from inside their eggs. The mother scrapes the sand from the nest and they break out of their eggs, using a special egg tooth which later drops off. Each baby is about the size of a small lizard.

The dash for the water

As soon as they hatch, the babies head for the water. They know how to swim straightaway! Sometimes the mother carries them down to the water in her mouth.

Baby crocodiles eat small worms, snails and insects.

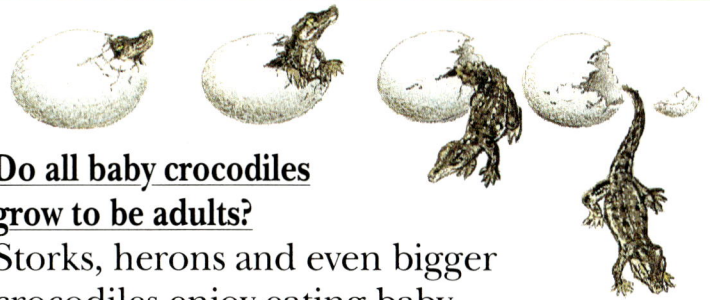

Do all baby crocodiles grow to be adults?

Storks, herons and even bigger crocodiles enjoy eating baby crocodiles. The parents may create a special nursery of river bank holes where they can guard their young from predators. Despite this care, only about two crocodiles will survive from each clutch of eggs.

The tropical forests of Africa...

Mandrills

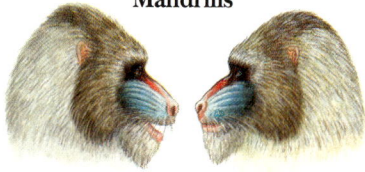

It rains a lot near the equator*. The hot, wet climate is just right for tropical rainforest*.

The jungle is dense and mysterious. It is difficult to see the animals because they are hidden by the thick leaves and branches. Monkeys, apes and birds live in the trees, while other animals prowl the forest floor.

de Brazza's monkey

Drill

In the Congo you might be lucky enough to meet a very rare animal: the okapi.

It looks a bit like a giraffe, though its neck is shorter. It is shy and easily frightened, running away at the slightest rustle of crushed leaves. Is a leopard about to attack? The okapi feeds on young leaves and twigs, buds and fruit. But it also eats grass, ferns and mushrooms. Its black tongue is so long and bendy it can even lick its own ears and eyes!

A baby okapi grows inside its mother for 14 months before it is born. Then it stays safely hidden in the bushes for two weeks, feeding on its mother's milk. After this it will forage in the forest for food. Only male okapis have horns.

Giant forest hogs are enormous.

This wild pig weighs up to 150 kilos. It was only discovered at the beginning of this century. Like a warthog, it wallows in mud to stop its skin drying out and cracking in the sun. It eats grass, leaves and fruits.

Giant forest hog

...are home to many wonderful creatures.

Bongos are big antelopes.
They have long horns, shaped like a lyre*. They are shy and like to live alone. Bongos usually hide in the undergrowth, but they will walk many miles to find their favourite food.

Many different monkeys live in the forest.
Diana monkeys are quick and lively. They eat fruit from the trees and fill the forest with their piercing cries. De Brazza monkeys are calmer and quieter. When there is danger, they keep quite still and silent. Mandrills are baboons. They live mainly on the ground. They have hidden pockets in their cheeks for storing extra food.

In the tropical rainforest*, apes swing on the long creepers, birds flit among the giant trees and a flying squirrel leaps from branch to branch.

Hornbill

Chimpanzee

Grey parrot

Flying squirrel

Okapi

Bongo

Congo peacock

Gorillas are strong but gentle.

Gorillas can be huge!

They can be three times as large as a man, but they are gentle giants. They eat only vegetables and leaves, chewing them up with their strong teeth.

You will find them in the tropical* forests and mountains of Africa, in groups of up to 30 males, females and babies.

Gorilla's foot

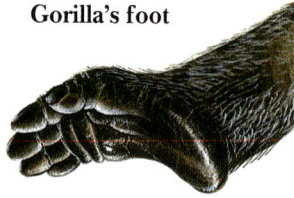

Gorilla's hand

They nibble all the time.

During the day they walk around the forest, and half the time they are eating leaves, berries, shoots and even bark. Mountain gorillas feed on wild celeries, thistles and nettles.

The oldest male silverback is the leader.

Gorillas are not fully grown until they are 15 years old. Only then does their black back change to silver-grey. The leader is strong but kind. He protects the rest of the group.

Gorillas are too heavy to swing in the trees, but they are fast and agile on the ground. They curl their hands and walk on their knuckles.

Baby gorillas are small and helpless.

A newborn gorilla weighs less than one and a half kilos, half the weight of a human baby. Its mother takes it with her wherever she goes. It relies on her for everything.

A baby gorilla stays with its mother until it is four years old.

The baby grows stronger and more active.

When it is about five weeks old, it begins to crawl. By four months it can walk on all fours and by eight and a half months it can stand upright. Others in the group look after the young gorilla and treat it gently.

Older gorillas look out for danger.

The mother teaches her young which plants to eat. Even when they are old enough to look after themselves, the young gorillas stay with the group for many years. When a young male becomes a silverback, he leaves the group and lives on his own until he can find his own territory* and females.

Chimpanzees are nimble and bright.

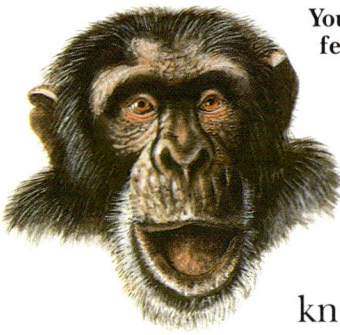

You can see what a chimpanzee is feeling from the expression on its face.

As soon as the sun rises, chimpanzees are up and about in search of food.

Chimpanzees are known for liking bananas, but they cannot always find a banana plantation. In the jungle, they eat fruits, buds, nuts and cereals. Sometimes they catch lizards, insects and even small monkeys.

Chimpanzees are good at solving problems.

If a chimp is thirsty and far from a stream, it chews up leaves to make a sponge. It pushes the sponge into the forks of branches to soak up water caught there. Then it squeezes the water into its mouth. Sometimes, a chimp will use a large leaf like a spoon, dipping it into water and drinking from it like a soup spoon. Chimpanzees are very fond of termites*. They will poke long stalks of grass into holes in the termites' nest. The termites climb on, and when the chimp pulls out the stalks he can lick off the termites.

These chimps have found a termites' nest.

A fresh nest every night

Chimpanzees like to build a platform of branches and leaves high in a tree, where they can sleep out of reach of predators*. Mothers sleep with their babies; the others sleep alone. Gorillas sleep on the ground, in nests of branches padded with leaves.

Life is hard in the African desert.

Deserts cover most of north and south-west Africa.

It is very hot during the day, and very cold at night. Rain is rare and conditions are harsh. It is surprising how many animals manage to live there.

Escaping the heat.
Lizards bury themselves in the sand and wait for the ants and beetles they eat.

Some lizards shelter in bushes or in the shade of a rock. Jerboas avoid the scorching ground by moving in jumps. Their tails help them to keep their balance.

Savanna gazelle

How do you drink when there is no water?
Many lizards get enough water from the insects and plants they eat. Jerboas and other rodents* get enough from the seeds they feed on.
Desert antelopes like springboks, oryxes and gazelles can last several months without drinking. They survive on the dew and sap from plants.

Ostriches are the largest birds, but they can't fly.
An ostrich measures 3 metres in height and weighs more than 150 kilos. They live in the desert and savannas* but stay close to waterholes* because they need to drink. Although ostriches cannot fly, they can run very fast – up to 150 kilometres an hour – as fast as a car on the motorway.

The male ostrich is a good father.
He lives with several females who all lay their eggs in the same nest. He guards the nest and takes it in turn with the females to sit on the eggs for 42 days. Each egg weighs a kilo and a half. The shell is so thick you would need a saw to open it. Luckily a baby ostrich has a special egg tooth to help him break out!

How do creatures survive the desert heat?

Baby ostriches grow a centimetre a day. As soon as they hatch, they leave the nest and begin to explore. If a hyena or jackal is spotted, the ostrich parents cry loudly, flap their wings and zigzag around to distract the enemy's attention. Meanwhile another ostrich rushes the chicks to a safe place.

Desert sidewinding viper

The sidewinding viper makes a strange pattern in the sand.

As it flicks its head and body sideways, hardly any of its belly touches the hot ground for long. It can dive beneath the sand where it waits, coiled up, with just its head showing. If a small rodent* passes, the snake will shoot out and snatch it. At night, the snake searches for prey* among the bushes and burrows.

The smallest fox of all lives in the desert.

Fennec foxes weigh less than a kilo and a half. They have long, sensitive ears which give them acute hearing. The soles of their feet are covered with protective hair so they can walk on the sand without getting burnt. In daytime they tend to remain inside their cool burrows. At night they go out hunting for rodents, lizards, birds and insects.

Oryxes, like sidewinding vipers and fennecs, are nocturnal.

Oryxes can tolerate very high temperatures.

During the mating season male oryxes fight noisy duels with their long thin horns. After mating, females go to the scrub at the edge of the desert to give birth. This happens during the rainy season when there is plenty of water for their babies to drink.

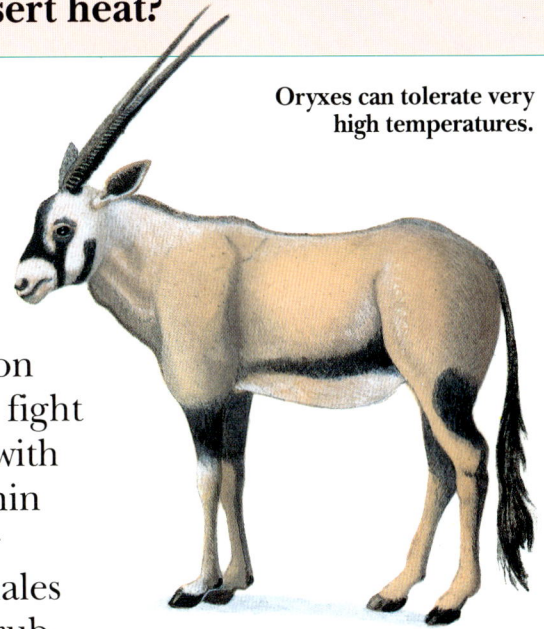

Oryxes can walk miles to find water.

But, like many desert animals, they need little to drink and they hardly sweat at all. They graze at night on succulent desert plants whose fruits or bulbs provide them with the moisture they need.

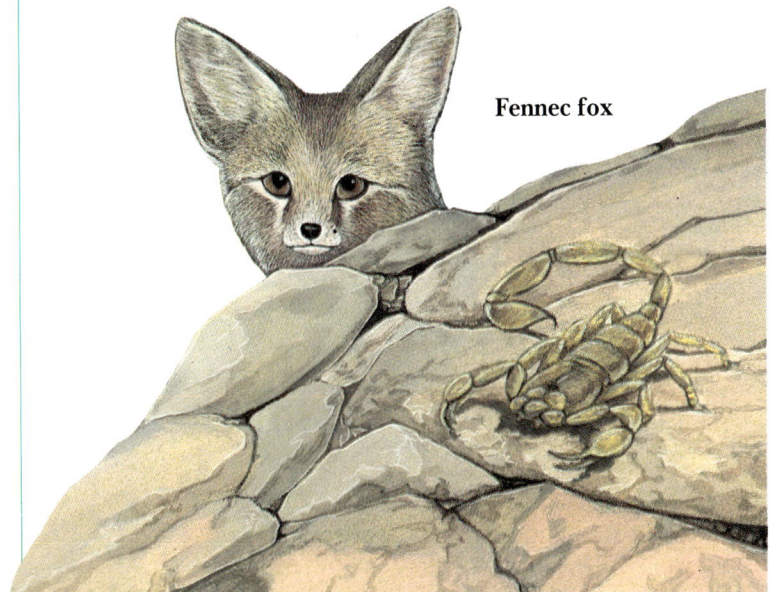

Fennec fox

Pandas live in China.

Snow leopards and pandas live in the high mountains of the Himalayas. Down below, in the tropical forests of South-East Asia, you will find big apes like the orang-utan and the biggest cat of all, the tiger.

One of the rarest animals
Scientists still aren't sure whether pandas are bears or raccoons but everyone agrees that they are in danger of dying out.

A diet of bamboo
Bamboo is the panda's staple diet. They bite off the bark with their teeth and carefully strip off the leaves with their front paws. They eat the leaves and suck the sweet juice inside the soft shoots. A sort of sixth finger acts like a thumb, helping them to hold the tiniest twig.

Pandas spend half their lives feeding.
They have to eat 12 hours a day to get the 12 kilos of bamboo they need. They also eat flowers like gentians, irises and crocuses. Sometimes they feed on dead rats. When they are full, they climb into a tree to rest.

They are shy and usually live on their own in the forest.
But in Spring they are ready to mate*. The males call out to attract a female. Sometimes two males will fight each other for the same female. A male and female spend a day or two together, getting to know each other, before they mate.

They are an endangered species.

Panda mothers are as cuddly as they look.

Four or five months after mating, the female panda gives birth in the fork of a tree. She can only look after one baby at a time, so if she has twins, she abandons the weaker one. For three months, until the baby learns to walk, the mother carries it with her wherever she goes. She rocks it and licks it tenderly and caresses it when it cries. She keeps it safe from leopards and wolves.

Baby pandas love playing.

Panda babies will slide down slopes, turn somersaults and hang upside down in trees. By the time they are a month old, they have their black 'socks, glasses and jacket'! They start eating bamboo shoots when they are six months old, but will continue to drink their mother's milk for a further two months.

There are just a thousand pandas left in the wild.

Even in nature reserves* their territory* is getting smaller and smaller. Farmers are destroying bamboo forests to make fields for their crops and to build villages. Pandas cannot move on to new territory because it too has been taken over by people, and so they are not getting enough to eat. Pandas could become extinct*.

A leopard which loves the snow

The snow leopard has a luxurious coat to keep out the bitter cold.

It lives up to 6,000 metres high among the frozen peaks of the Himalayas where there is snow all year round. Its magnificent coat is very thick, especially in winter.

You can recognize it by its light grey fur, spotted with black rings.

Snow leopards

Its long tail helps to keep it warm.

When a snow leopard is tired, it curls up with its long tail round its neck like a scarf, and goes to sleep. When it is on the move, its tail acts as a balance as it leaps from rock to rock.

Its big feet are like snow shoes.

A snow leopard has wide paws which stop it sinking into the snow. They are covered with long hair so they don't slide on the ice.

A snow leopard attacks a mountain goat.

What do they find to eat in the snowy mountains?

In summer snow leopards hunt for prey* in the high grassy pastures. They attack gorals and wild goats such as markhors. These animals too have thick heavy coats. In winter snow leopards move lower down the mountain. They steal into the forests in search of stags, wild boars and martens.

Even the huge yaks fear that their young may be attacked by a snow leopard.

Yaks

Snow leopards are an endangered species*.

So many have been hunted for their fur that there are fewer than a thousand left in the wild. It is now illegal to hunt them.

Markhor

Gorals

Snub-nosed monkeys and moon bears live in the Himalayas.

Snub-nosed monkeys keep to the trees.

They climb down to the ground only to eat and drink. They live in groups and roam about the forests looking for leaves. They also feed on fruit, buds, bamboo shoots, insects, eggs and even birds. Snub-nosed monkeys have practically no nose. They have a beautiful gold-brown coat whose thick fur protects them from the snow. They are also called rhinopithecus monkeys, and are so rare that little is known about them.

Keep out of the way of moon bears!

A snub-nosed monkey

The people who live in the Himalayan mountains are terrified of coming face to face with a moon bear on a narrow path. These bears are highly strung and will attack people and their horses. They live in forests in the high mountains, at about 1,500 to 3,000 metres. They are called moon bears because of the crescent-shaped patch of white fur on their chests.

Moon bears are clever.

They are good swimmers and excellent tree-climbers. When the weather is bad, they will sleep in a sheltered place high in a tree. In winter they will gather grass and twigs to make a den in a sunny spot on the snow. There they can rest and dry their fur.

A family of bears

Unlike other bears which like to live alone, the male moon bear lives with a female and sometimes with its cubs.

Moon bears eat everything.

They are omnivorous*. They feed on fruit and nuts as well as ants, larvae*, meat and even rotting carcasses*.

In the jungle you can't see the sky!

Liana* creepers and the branches of enormous trees arch overhead to form a green canopy. Plants and trees make such dense growth in Borneo that you need an axe to cut your way through the jungle. Flying frogs, squirrels and lizards glide through the air. The orang-utan, who walks upright like a man, spends most of its life in the trees.

Orang-utans throw branches down at their enemies.

Orang-utans really enjoy their food.

In the forests of Indonesia they will walk for hours in search of a bunch of lychees, some wild figs, or a durian, a kind of big, spiny, smelly fruit which they love. They will only select the very best. They are fussy eaters.

The male orang-utan lives on his own,

except in the mating season, when he broadcasts his presence to females for many kilometres around with a long, piercing scream. Males are twice as big as females. and the most dominant* have rolls of fat around their cheeks and foreheads to make them look bigger. Baby orang-utans are small and delicate. They have to cling to their mother all the time in case they get lost in the jungle.

Orang-utans swing slowly from branch to branch.

They lean down to drink very carefully – they can't swim!

Some monkeys live on the ground, others prefer the trees.

Gibbons swing through the trees...

...30 metres up...

...and can leap across an 8-metre clearing in one bound!

Who's up there in the tree tops?
A gibbon, the acrobat of the apes! With its enormously long arms, it dangles like a trapeze artist, and swings from tree to tree. But it can lose its balance and fall down.

Proboscis monkeys have long noses.

Gibbons live in many Asian forests.

Siamangs can blow up a sac of stretchy skin beneath their chin.

Gibbons are very loving.
A male and a female, or sometimes a male and two females live with their children as a family group.

Every morning they screech a noisy greeting across the jungle.
Then the whole family sets out to look for food. They pick fruit, leaves, flowers and buds. They catch insects and steal birds' eggs. In the afternoon they will stop for a nap, and at sunset they will return to their own territory* to sleep.

Female gibbons have a baby every two or three years.
Young gibbons stay with the family until they are adult, about eight years old.

Proboscis monkeys have big, droopy noses.
Sometimes their noses are so long they get in the way when they are feeding on leaves and fruits. Proboscis monkeys live in groups among the mangrove* swamps of Borneo.

Macaques are well organized.
They don't squabble and they work together to defend themselves. They walk in a long line, one in front of the other. They groom each other to get rid of parasites* and to relax.

Macaque mothers are patient. They teach their babies everything.

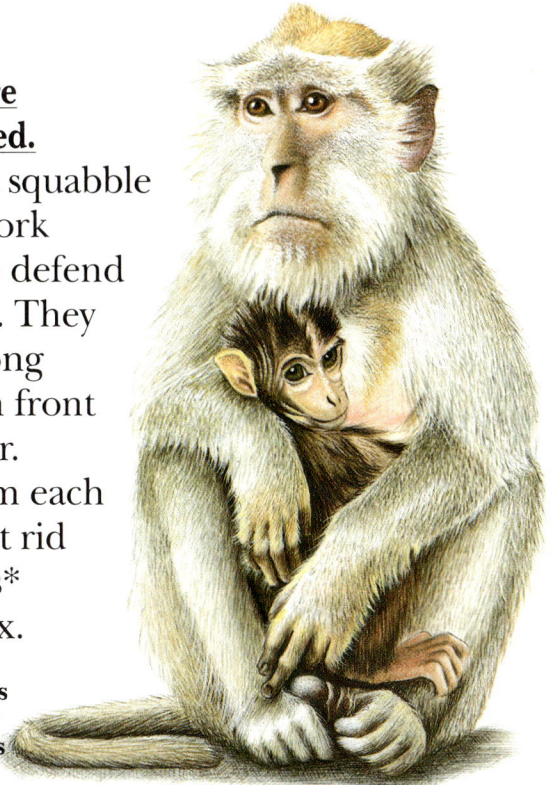

Tigers stalk silently through the jungle.

A tiger and a tigress sometimes hunt together.
When they see prey*, they will creep slowly towards it until they are near enough to leap and seize it with their powerful jaws. A tiger may even attack a buffalo, but it must watch out. Buffaloes are brave fighters.

Tigers will also hunt peacocks and turtles. And they will dip a paw into a river to catch a fish.

Ravenous and crafty

A tiger eats about 15 kilos of meat a day. When it has killed its prey, it may drag the carcass* several hundred metres to a sheltered place. If it cannot finish it off, it will cover the flesh with leaves, or hide it under water to prevent the smell attracting another meat-eater. No tiger wants to have its food stolen!

Tiger cubs must learn to hunt.

Tigers are the largest of all cats. They can weigh over 250 kilos.

Despite its size, the tiger creeps silently through the undergrowth, ready to pounce on deer, antelopes and rabbits!

Tigers live alone until they mate*.

The female tiger spreads her smelly urine all over her territory*. It will attract a male.

Look out, tiger! The elephant may charge you.

The male smells the female. For a few days, they hunt together and share their prey*. Then they mate* and the male often leaves. The cubs are born a hundred days later in a den made by the mother.

Tiger cubs learn to hunt as they play.

They love stalking each other and pouncing on their mother's tail. By the time they are six months old, they can catch birds. Then they begin to hunt with their mother. When they are two years old they are ready to leave.

A young tiger makes its own territory*.

It defends it against other tigers. It scratches the ground and slashes trees to let other tigers know they must keep away, and marks the border of the territory with its urine.

Australia has many extraordinary animals.

Spiny anteaters and duck-billed platypuses are mammals*, like sheep or goats, but they lay eggs! Kangaroos and koalas are marsupials* that carry their babies in a pouch on their tummy.

What's this animal hopping along like a big rabbit? It's called the greater rabbit-eared bandicoot.

Kangaroos bound across the desert.

The biggest kangaroos can jump 10 metres in a hop and travel as fast as 50 kilometres an hour. Wallabies are the kangaroo's smaller cousins.

Growing up in a pouch.

When a kangaroo is born it is only about one centimetre long. It's blind and helpless but it crawls through its mother's fur and into her pouch where it can suck milk from her teat. As it grows bigger and stronger, it climbs in and out of her pouch. When it is eight months old it leaves its cosy home. But a new baby will soon take its place in the pouch.

At night the desert echoes with howls.

As one howl dies away, another follows. They are made by dingoes talking to each other. These wild dogs look like wolves and live in packs. They hunt rabbits and small game.

The moloch, or mountain devil, looks like a dragon, but it's actually no bigger than your hand. It eats ants.

The shingle-backed lizard, 45 centimetres long, is also quite harmless. It has a piercing whistle and it sticks out its blue tongue when it is attacked.

The frilled lizard also whistles if it's cornered. When it is cornered it spreads out a fold of skin around its neck to make itself look fierce.

Frilled lizard

54

The duck-billed platypus is the oddest.

Koalas only eat eucalyptus.

They eat a kilo of eucalyptus leaves a night. At mating time the male koala is fierce. It patrols its territory*, ready to chase away other males. The female has one baby a year. She carries it in her pouch until it is seven months old. Then it moves around and clings onto her back.

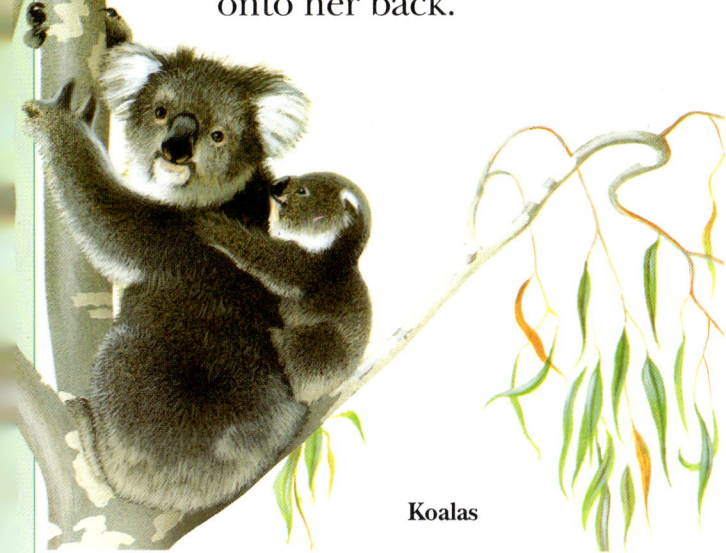

The lyre* bird spreads out its tail like a peacock.

Kookaburras are related to kingfishers.

Koalas

What has an otter's body and a duck's head?

A duck-billed platypus. It lives on crabs, larvae* and small fish. The female lays two eggs in a small burrow in the river bank. They hatch in a week. The mother has no nipples but produces milk which seeps from her glands* through her skin. The babies lap it up.

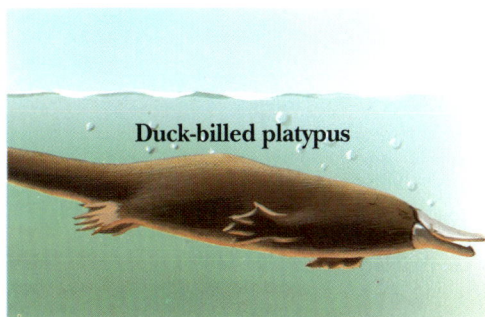

The dawn chorus in Australia is unique.

Parrots and lorikeets come in every colour. The kookaburra laughs, and the bellbird makes a ringing sound just like a bell.

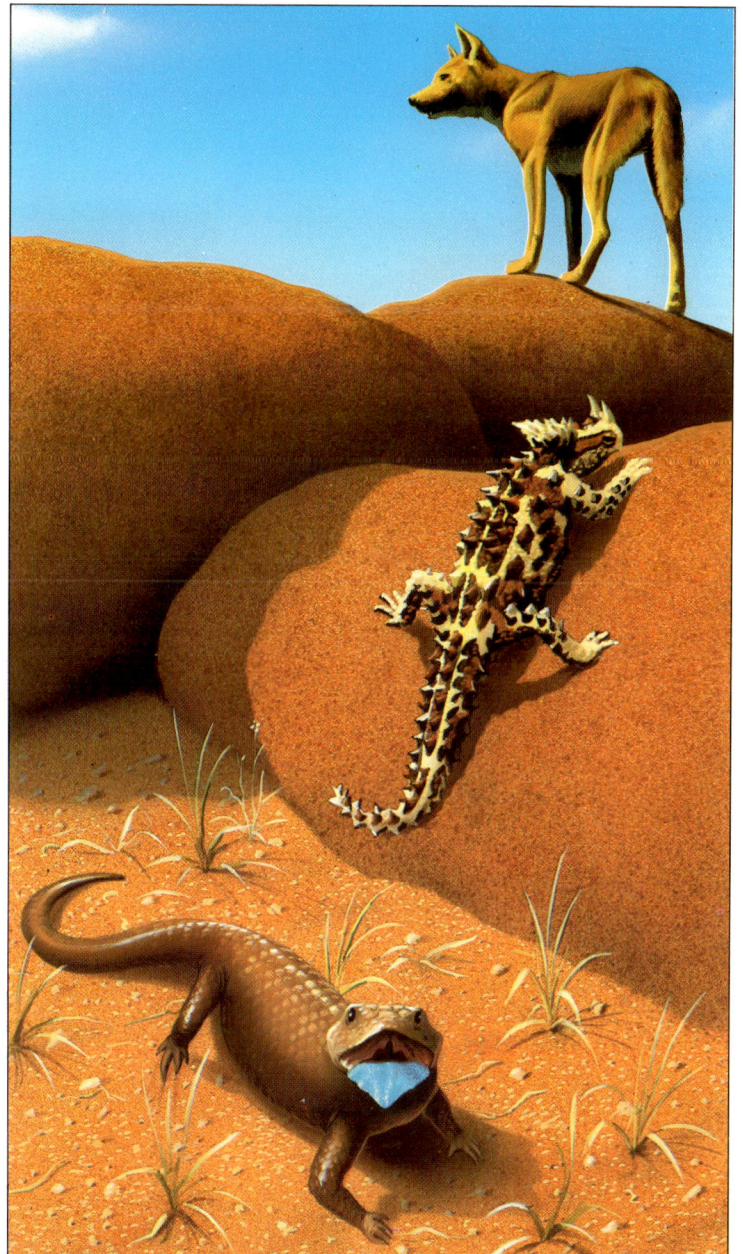

Duck-billed platypus

A dingo scans the desert. It doesn't notice the moloch and shingle-backed lizard behind it.

The animals on tropical islands are not seen anywhere else.

Mouse lemur

Madagascar is a big island just off the south-east coast of Africa. It is the home of the lemur, ancestor to the monkey.

Islands like Madagascar, the Seychelles, the Antilles and the Galapagos have a range of extraordinary reptiles and birds which attract visitors from all over the world.

Mouse lemurs and sifakas are two of many different lemur species which live in Madagascar.

Mouse lemurs hunt at night.

They have big, shiny eyes for seeing in the dark. They feed on fruit, insects and other small animals. They growl as they move and snap at any bird of prey* which attacks them. During the long, dry season, they hibernate* for eight months, surviving on the fat stored in their tails.
Sifakas are large, agile lemurs that jump from one tree trunk to another. They have scent glands* beneath their chins and mark their territory* by rubbing scent onto the branches of trees.

The macaco lemur is endangered*.

The male has thick, silky black fur and the female is reddish-orange. They spend a lot of time basking in the sun. They love bananas and mangoes and are so tame, they will take food straight from your hand.

Aye-ayes are lemurs with amazingly long middle fingers. They grub out larvae* from beneath the bark of trees.

Turtles spend most of their lives in the sea.

Turtles only come onto land to lay their eggs.

As the sun sets, you can watch the females crawling over the sand. They swim very fast in water, but on land they move painfully slowly. Far up the beach, out of reach of the high tide, the female turtle digs a small hole. She lays about a hundred eggs in it. She covers the nest carefully with sand and returns to the sea.

Few baby turtles survive.

The eggs stay warm in the hot sand and hatch after two months. The tiny turtles instinctively start crawling back to the sea. Before they reach the safety of the water, however, seabirds hovering overhead dive down and scoop many of them up. Most are eaten, and only a small number survive.

The largest animal in the world...

Whales and dolphins swim in the sea, but they are not fish. They come to the surface to breathe air and they feed their babies with milk. They belong to a group of mammals* called cetaceans.

Some species of whales feed on fish and squid, chewing them with their teeth. Most of the largest whales have no teeth at all.

Sperm whales can stay underwater for an hour and a half!

They dive deeper than any other whale in their search for squid and fish. They can dive as deep as a kilometre.

Killer whales are expert hunters.

They swim in packs, their large dorsal* fins slicing through the surface of the water. They attack sharks, seals, dolphins and even large whales. They eat a huge amount, but they don't attack people.

The sperm whale is the largest toothed whale. Killer whales are not whales, but a sort of large dolphin. The beluga is dark grey when it is born but becomes white when it is four or five years old.

Dolphins

Killer whale

Sperm whale

Beluga, or white whale

The narwhal has just one long tooth, like a horn, to defend itself.

The blue whale is the largest and heaviest animal that has ever lived!

Dolphins can swim very fast – up to 50 kilometres an hour. They leap out of the water to take breaths of air.

Some are 30 metres long and the weight of 30 elephants. Like the humpback whale and the great right whale, blue whales have no teeth. Instead they have rows of horny plates called baleen.

They swallow huge gulps of tiny plants and animals, called plankton*.

The food is filtered through the rows of baleen plates which hang down from the top of the whale's mouth.

Blue whales eat 1,000 kilos of tiny animals in a single meal. Baleen whales also need vast quantities of food.

Whales breathe in through two nostrils or blow-holes on top of their heads. But first they blow out a cloud of steamy, stale air!

Humpback whale

Bowhead whale

Fin whale

Great right whale

Blue whale

The biggest baby on our planet

A dolphin calf is born.

It rides on its mother's back.

The mother dolphin suckles her calf for 16 months.

A newborn blue whale weighs 5 tonnes*.
It is 7 metres long. Its mother has to coax it to the surface to take its first vital breaths of air. The calf suckles* underwater. The milk squirts straight into its mouth from its mother's teats. It drinks up to 450 litres of milk a day.

The whale calf doubles its birth weight in a week, so it puts on four and a half kilos every hour! The baby is born in warm seas near the equator*. Before it can return to the cold polar seas, it must build up a thick layer of fatty blubber. The long journey to the polar seas takes several months.

The mother whale protects her calf. She will risk her own life to save it from attack.

Whales and dolphins have their own language.

Whales and dolphins are very sociable.

They live in family groups, called schools. Sometimes several hundred live together with one animal acting as leader.

Why do they leap out of the water?

To raise the alarm, to keep in contact in rough seas, or sometimes to attract females. The young jump just for fun!

Dolphins are very intelligent.

They can be trained to help divers fetch objects from the ocean bed. And they are quick to learn tricks based on their natural movements. Have you seen them balancing upright on their tails and leaping through hoops? Tame killer whales and dolphins perform in aquariums. They are fun to watch, but they are not happy and they don't live long in captivity.

A dolphin

Whistles, groans, chirps and clicks...

These are the sort of sounds whales and dolphins use to communicate with each other. They make other sounds as well, too high-pitched for us to hear. Dolphins and toothed whales have poor eyesight but they have excellent hearing. Like bats, they use high-pitched sounds to detect if anything is in their way. The returning echoes tell them the shape of the object and its distance away.

Sea-lions

Many other mammals* live in the sea.

Seals and their cousins spend only part of their lives on land or on ice-floes*. Their skin is covered with short, sleek fur, and they hunt fish, crabs, shellfish and seabirds. They can stay underwater for up to 20 minutes.

The monk seal lives in the Mediterranean Sea.

The smallest seal is the ringed seal.

The biggest sea mammal is the sea-elephant. It can weigh 4 tonnes*, and can measure 5 metres from nose to tail.

The grey seal lives off the coasts of Britain.

The male elephant seal can inflate his nose like a trunk.

How can you tell a sea-lion from a seal?

A sea-lion's ears are on the outside of its head. A seal's are not.

The sea is full of exotic creatures...

Most fish live in shallow seas or near the surface of the sea where they can feed on plankton*. The types of fish found in the sea vary depending on the temperature of the water and the kind of plants growing there. Coral reefs teem with brilliantly coloured marine life including clownfish, damsel-fish and angel fish.

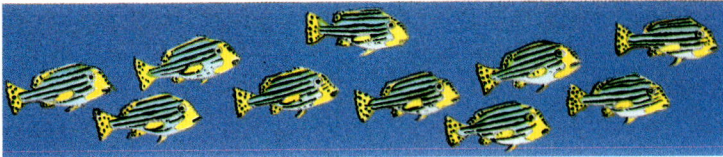

A shark's dorsal* fin slices through the water.
It needs its dorsal fin to keep it steady in the water. It is a terrifying sight and perhaps the only sign that the shark is there. The shark uses its other fins to help it turn.

Sharks are fast, silent hunters.
Their powerful tails propel them forward through the water. Some sharks eat plankton, but most catch fish, squid and shellfish.
The great white shark attacks turtles, sea-birds and even other sharks. It leaps out of the water to snatch seals and sea-lions. It tears them apart with its rows of terrible teeth. When a tooth wears out, a new one replaces it. A shark goes through thousands of teeth in its life.

Manta rays are the largest flat fish.
Some are as wide as 7 metres and weigh almost 2,000 kilos. They look as if they are flying under the water.

Black tip reef shark

Tiger shark

Marlin

Manta ray

Hammerhead
shark

Turtle

Puffer fish

Moray eel

Barracuda

Games and activities, a quiz, intriguing facts, sayings, a glossary, followed by the index

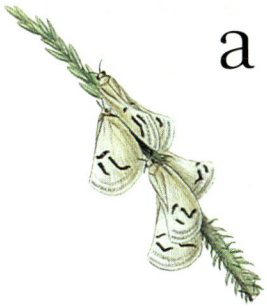

■ Did you know?

Who were the elephant's ancestors?
The moeritherium, which lived over 60 million years ago. Slowly, generation by generation, its descendants, which included the dinotherium and the mastodon, grew bigger and bigger. Their noses gradually grew longer, until they finally developed into trunks. Two of their upper teeth grew into tusks.

Dinotherium

Mastodon

Mammoths were hairy cousins of the elephant.
They first appeared on Earth 10 million years ago. The complete, frozen bodies of some ancient mammoths have been found in the Arctic ice.

Lions and elephants once roamed across what we now call the Sahara Desert.
Even as recently as 2000 years ago, North Africa had more rain and more plants and trees than it has now.

Indian elephants are different from African elephants.
Indian elephants have smaller ears and a rounder head than their African cousins. They live in the dense, steamy tropical forests of southern Asia.

Helpful and strong
People in India traditionally use the intelligence and strength of female elephants to help them with hard and heavy work. Older elephants help to teach younger ones how to do the work.

Elephants live to a great age.
They usually die of hunger when they are about 50 to 60 years old. By then their teeth have worn away.

In Asia, only male elephants have visible tusks.

In India each working elephant has her own keeper, or mahout, who always looks after her.

Elephant school
The elephant learns how to carry her master and to understand his commands. Later, she learns how to lift heavier and heavier tree trunks. When she's finished learning, she's put to work in the forest where it's too swampy for bulldozers.

Black rhinos and white rhinos are really the same colour!
Only the shape of their mouth is different. White rhinos have large, straight mouths for grazing on grass. Black rhinos have pointed mouths for browsing on leaves.

What a little monkey you are!
When grown-ups say that they mean you are being cheeky and naughty. But when monkeys or apes call out and jump up and down, clapping their hands, they aren't fooling around: they are talking to each other and showing each other whether they are happy, friendly or cross.

Apes have long arms.
Their arms are longer than their legs. Unlike monkeys, they have no tail. Apes are our closest relatives.

Humans, monkeys, apes and lemurs belong to the same family: the primates.
They all have hands which can grip and eyes that can see colour and measure distance. Monkeys and apes have feet which can grip too. They use them to grasp branches.

■ Did you know?

Red pandas live in China and Nepal. They are about the size and shape of a pet cat. The fur on their back

is thick and red, and their tummy is black. There are more Red pandas than Giant pandas but they are shy and not often seen. They live in forests and use their claws to climb trees. They eat bamboo shoots and fruit, varying their diet with insects, eggs and small birds.

In ancient Egypt, crocodiles were worshipped as gods. In the Pharaohs' time a city, Crocodilopolis, was built in their honour. Priests put gold bracelets on their arms, and fed them cakes and honey.

What are crocodile tears? People say they are pretend crying because crocodiles have tears in their eyes only if they yawn, or are washing sea salt from their eyes.

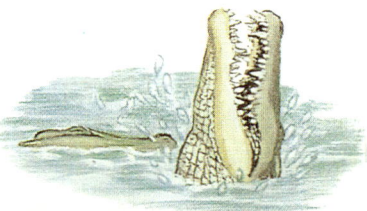

People used to capture bears and teach them tricks. They would travel from town to town with their dancing bears. Bears are intelligent and learn quickly, but, like all wild animals, they hate being in captivity.

Sun bears love to sunbathe! They have sleek fur like a seal, and the palms of their large paws are hairless to help them cling to the palm trees they climb. They eat coconuts and sugar-cane, and lie along a branch basking in the hot sun.
They come from Malaya and are the smallest of all bears. They weigh less than 65 kilos and are only about a metre long.

Nile crocodile

Crocodiles are becoming very rare. They have been hunted for their skins, which are valuable. They are now protected and live in reserves.

Central American cayman

Skins used for expensive handbags, belts and shoes should not come from wild crocodiles, caymans, gharials or alligators, but from crocodiles raised on special farms.

■ **Did you know?**

Wild cats have beautiful, patterned fur.
It helps them hide while they stalk their prey. Leopards and lynxes have dappled fur, tigers have stripes. They can merge into their surroundings, unheard and unseen, until they're ready to pounce. Their strong muscles and powerful jaws mean they can kill prey twice their own size. Cats kill what they need to eat. Then they rest.

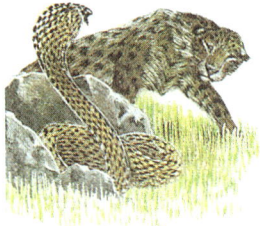

Why do cats have green eyes?
They have special reflectors at the back of their eyes which catch the light and reflect it forward.

Cats have enemies too.
They are careful to avoid elephants, which may charge them and trample them to death, particularly if the adults are protecting baby elephants. They watch out for crocodiles when they go to the water to drink, and they fear snakes which might spit poison at them or squeeze them to death. But the big cats' greatest enemies are people who hunt them for their fur.

In the dry savanna, lions hide in the grass to wait for antelope and giraffes.

Wildlife alert!
The snow leopard, the Bengal tiger and almost all the big cats are in danger of dying out. Lions are safe from hunters because their fur is not considered beautiful, but their habitats are under threat from development.

A leopard sometimes hides in a tree so it can drop down on its unsuspecting prey.

Only lions live in family groups.
The lionesses hunt together and bring back food for the lion and cubs. Although the lion may seem lazy, his job is to protect the whole family.

Have you ever seen an eagle attacking its prey?
It hovers in the sky with its wings outstretched. It sees a rat. Suddenly it dives towards the ground and drops onto its prey. It seizes it in its talons and soars up into the sky again. The eagle can carry heavy prey into the mountain peaks where it has its eyrie.

■ Quiz

Can you answer these questions? The answers are at the bottom of this page.

1. Chimps like to eat
a) grass
b) mice
c) termites

2. Which bear does not hibernate?
a) brown bear
b) black bear
c) sun bear

3. Which is the biggest penguin?
a) royal penguin
b) emperor penguin
c) pygmy penguin

4. Which bird does not build a nest?
a) ostrich
b) eagle
c) emperor penguin

5. How much does a newborn polar bear cub weigh?
a) 700 grammes
b) one and a half kilos
c) 5 kilos

6. Which is the biggest of these bears?
a) sun bear
b) spectacled bear
c) polar bear

7. Which is the smallest bear?
a) moon bear
b) brown bear
c) sun bear

8. Which is the biggest cat?
a) ocelot
b) lion
c) Siberian tiger

9. Which bird helps elephants to get rid of their parasites?
a) plover
b) tick-bird
c) ibis

10. What irritates rhinos most?
a) insects
b) crocodiles
c) lions

■ True or false?

1. Elephants are afraid of mice.
2. Baby elephants suck their trunks.
3. There are elephant cemeteries.
4. Bracelets are made with hairs from an elephant's tail.
5. African elephants cannot be trained.
6. Elephants walk in a long line, each holding the tail of the one in front.
7. You can tell how old an elephant is by looking at its teeth.
8. An elephant can run as fast as 100 kph.

Answers

Quiz
1c, 2c, 3b, 4c, 5a, 6c, 7b, 8c, 9b, 10a

True or false
1. True
2. True, just like you do when you suck your thumb.
3. False. It is a legend. People thought it was true because they found the carcasses of a whole herd which had got stuck in a swamp.
4. True
5. False, but they are more difficult to train than Indian elephants.
6. True
7. True
8. False. It runs at 35 kph.

■ Who's who?

Serval

Albino tiger

Margay

Jaguar

Leopard

Black jaguar

Pampas cat

Ocelot

Jaguar

Pampas cat

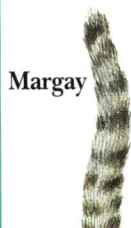
Margay

Serval

Ocelot

Leopard

Albino tiger

Black jaguar

■ Did you know?

Sloth bears love eating termites, and will break into their nests and lick out the insects with their tongues. The terrible noise they make doing this can be heard over 200 metres away, making them easy prey for hunters.

Whales are found in oceans all over the world.

In summer some migrate to the colder oceans near the North and South Poles where there is plenty of food. In winter they move into warmer water closer to the equator, where they mate and give birth to their young.

Killer whales have huge appetites.

Scientists once found the remains of 11 seals and 13 porpoises in the stomach of a whale! Killer whales prey on sharks, seals, dolphins and birds as well as on squid and fish. A group of killer whales will even attack a large whale, which does not stand a chance against those agile killers with their rows of fearsome teeth. But don't worry, killer whales do not attack people.

A 19th-century whaling-ship

Save the whales!

Until a few hundred years ago there were many whales of all kinds. Then people started hunting them. There are now so few of some species, they are almost extinct. For the past few years some countries have banned whaling, and whale populations have started to grow again. But Japan, Norway and Russia still have whaling fleets and so the whales are still in danger.

Why do people hunt whales?

In the past, the body of a whale provided lots of things humans found useful. The blubber was melted down to provide oil.

A catcher-ship drags its prey alongside.

Before electricity, whale oil was used as fuel in lamps, and was made into margarine and soap. Baleen was used for umbrella spokes and whale meat was eaten.

This factory-ship hoists the whale on board, where it is tied fast to the deck.

There is no need to hunt whales today.

People no longer need whale oil, because they have electricity. In Japan, whale meat was once cheap, but now it is a luxury. Only the rich can afford to buy it and they can eat other food instead. All the things which people once got from whales can now be made artificially.

Carving on a sperm whale's tooth

Did you know?

Walruses are cousins of the seal. They have two huge tusks which they use to dig for shellfish on the sea-bottom and to haul themselves on to ice-floes.

Walruses use their flippers as legs when they are on land.
They push their tummies off the ground and walk.

The dorsal fin of a killer whale

The tail of a blue whale

Whales cannot survive out of water.
Although they breathe air, they cannot live long on land. Without water to support them, the weight of their body crushes them to death.

What are krill?
They are tiny shrimps which blue whales and other baleen whales love to eat. But people have started fishing krill too. If people catch too many there won't be enough for the whales.

Some whales travel thousands of miles for their food.
Krill and plankton thrive in cold icy waters. Whales swim to the Antarctic or Arctic in summer to feed on them.

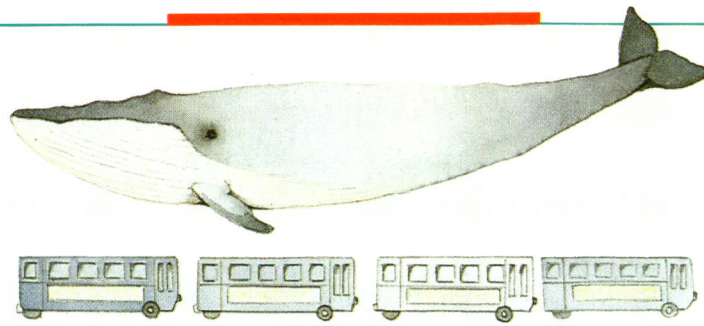

The blue whale is the world's largest animal. Some are 30 metres long, the length of four coaches parked one behind the other.

Skeleton of a fin whale

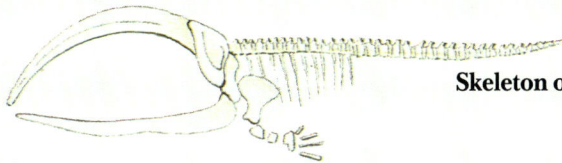

Skeleton of a right whale

Many animals have already become extinct.
Dinosaurs, mammoths and many other animals became extinct thousands of years ago. And in the last few hundred years many animals have become extinct because they have been hunted by people. They include 17 kinds of bears, five kinds of wolves and foxes, four kinds of cats, ten kinds of cattle, sheep, goats and antelopes and three kinds of deer. Many of these animals were killed for their fur, wool or skins.

These products may be thought beautiful or fashionable – but crocodile skin looks better on crocodiles!

Some animals thrive alongside people!
Mice, rats, pigeons and cockroaches are just a few of the animals that live off our food or our rubbish. Foxes, grey squirrels and raccoons are becoming common city-dwellers.

Some unexpected guests
You might be surprised by the animals you see in some cities.

In India, sacred cows wander freely about the streets.

In Florida, alligators have been found in swimming pools. The marshes where they used to live were drained and built on by people. Now the alligators are breeding in the sewers.

In Turkey, eagles live in the tops of old houses.

In Australia, opossums come into suburbs and towns looking for rubbish.

Elk sometimes stray into Moscow in Russia and Helsinki in Finland.

Big cat: Large member of the cat family. Jaguars, leopards, lions, tigers and ocelots are all big cats.
to Browse: feed on leaves, twigs, bark and shoots of trees and bushes.

Camouflage: the colour and patterns of an animal's skin or fur which help it match its surroundings.
Carcass: the dead body or remains of an animal, especially one that has been killed for food.
Clutch: a group of eggs which are incubated and hatch together.
Coniferous: describes the kinds of trees which produce their seeds in cones. Many coniferous trees have needle-like leaves which stay on the tree all year round.
Corpse: the dead body of an animal.

Domesticated: tamed and reared by people.
Dominant: ruling or leading. The strongest member of a group often dominates the rest.

Dorsal: situated on the back. Whales, dolphins and fish have dorsal fins to stop them rolling in the water.

Endangered: in danger or threatened. When a whole species of plant or animal is threatened with extinction it is said to be an endangered species.
Equator: An imaginary line around the middle of the Earth.
to Evaporate: to change from a liquid to a vapour or gas. When a liquid evaporates, it takes heat from its surroundings and cools them down.
Extinct: no longer existing. When all the plants or animals in a particular species have died, the species is said to be extinct.

Gland: structure in the body which produces a special substance, such as hormones or a strong-smelling liquid.
to Graze: to feed mainly on grass.

Habitat: the natural home of a particular plant or animal.
to Hibernate: to spend the winter asleep.

Ice-floe: a lump of floating ice.
to Incubate: to keep eggs warm until the young inside are ready to hatch. Most birds incubate their eggs by sitting on them.

Larva: an early stage in the life cycle of an insect or other animal which will look quite different when it becomes an adult. Caterpillars, for example, grow into moths or butterflies.
Liana: long creeper produced by a climbing tropical plant.
Lyre: an old musical instrument rather like a harp.

Mammal: member of a group of animals which feed their babies on milk produced by the mother. Most mammals have hair and give birth to fully-developed young.
Mangrove: tropical trees which grow in swampy ground at the mouth of rivers.
Marsupial: an animal group in which the female has a pouch to carry her young before they are fully developed.

to Mate: two animals mate when a male and female come together to produce young.

to Migrate: to move from place to place according to the season of the year.

Minerals: chemicals which animals need to eat to be healthy.

Muzzle: projecting part of animal's face including mouth and nose.

Nature reserve: area of land in which farming is limited and animals are protected.

Omnivore: an animal which eats plants and animals.

Oxygen: a gas which all plants and animals need to live. We breathe our oxygen from the air but fish get it from water.

Pack-ice: area of ice and water with many ice-floes.

Parasite: plant or animal that lives and feeds on a host plant or animal.

Plankton: Tiny plants and animals drifting in the sea.

Prairie: large area of natural grassland in North America.

Predator: An animal that hunts other animals for food.

Prey: an animal that is hunted for food.

Protected species: kind of animal or plant which you cannot harm or kill without legal permission.

Rainforest: tropical forest that grows where there is plenty of rain all year round.

Reptile: a large group of animals which includes snakes, turtles, lizards and crocodiles. They are covered with scales and rely on the Sun's heat to warm their bodies.

Rodent: a small mammal with large gnawing teeth. Mice, rats, squirrels and jerboas are all rodents.

Savanna: area of tropical grassland in South America, Africa or Australia.

Species: group of animals whose members are closely related and can breed with each other.

Suckle: to drink milk from the mother. Mammal babies suckle from their mother.

Termite: a tropical insect which lives in large groups. The nests form big mounds, taller than a person.

Territory: area of ground in which an animal and its family hunt or feed. Some animals mark the borders of their territory with scent or urine to warn off intruders.

Tonne: 1,000 kilos

Tropics: areas on each side of the equator where the weather is always hot and often very wet.

Waterhole: shallow pond, often in a dry riverbed, where animals come to drink.

Here is a list of more books you could read. Ask your library to help you find them, or visit your local bookshop.

Oxford Illustrated Encyclopedia of the Natural World
edited by Dr Malcolm Coe

Usborne Living World Encyclopedia
by Leslie Colvin and Emma Speare

Philip's Wildlife Atlas
by Robin Kerrod and John Sidworthy

Philip's Environment Atlas
by David Wright

Children's Atlas of Endangered Animals
by John Malam

Earth Watch
by Penny Horton

Vanishing Species – Green Issues
by Miles Barton

How Nature Works
by David Burne

Discovering Life on Earth
by David Attenborough

Polar Regions – **Our Green World**
by Barbara James

A for Antarctica
by Meredith Hooper

Antarctica – **The Living World**
by Sally Morgan and Pauline Lalor

Rainforest – **The Living World**
by Sally Morgan and Pauline Lalor

What is a Rainforest?
by Dr Philip Whitfield

Rainforest – **New View**
by Fiona MacDonald

Deserts – **Our Green World**
by Ewan McLeish

Seas and Oceans – **New View**
by David Lambert

Ocean Life – **Wildlife Rescue**
by David Cook

Oceans – **Wildside**
by Nick Davies

Grasslands – **The Young Geographer Investigates**
by Terry Jennings

Life in the Islands; People, Plants, Wildlife
by Rosanne Hooper

The entries in **bold** refer to whole chapters on the subject.